First Facts™

Exploring the Animal Kingdom

Birds

king penguins

by Adele Richardson

Consultant:
Robert T. Mason
Professor of Zoology, J. C. Braly Curator of Vertebrates
Oregon State University
Corvallis, Oregon

Capstone
press

Mankato, Minnesota

First Facts is published by Capstone Press,
151 Good Counsel Drive, P.O. Box 669, Mankato, Minnesota 56002.
www.capstonepress.com

Library of Congress Cataloging-in-Publication Data
Richardson, Adele, 1966–
    Birds / by Adele Richardson.
      p. cm.—(First facts. Exploring the animal kingdom)
    Includes bibliographical references and index.
    Contents: Birds—Birds are vertebrates—Birds are warm-blooded—Bodies of birds—Birds
have feathers—How birds breathe—What birds eat—Young birds—Amazing but true!—Compare
the main animal groups.
      ISBN 0-7368-2621-1 (hardcover)
      ISBN 0-7368-4943-2 (paperback)
      1. Birds—Juvenile literature. [1. Birds.] I. Title. II. Series.
QL676.2.R525 2005
598—dc22   2003027249

Editorial credits
Erika L. Shores, editor; Linda Clavel, designer; Kelly Garvin, photo researcher;
    Eric Kudalis, product planning editor

Photo credits
Ann & Rob Simpson, cover (middle left), 9
Bruce Coleman Inc./H. Schrempp, 10; J. C. Carton, 16; John Hyde, 6–7; Tom Ulrich, 18–19
Creatas, cover (bottom left)
Dave Watts/naturepl.com, 15
Digital Vision/Joel Simon, 1
Dwight R. Kuhn, 17
Eda Rogers, 20
McDonald Wildlife Photography, 11, 12–13
Stockbyte, cover (top left, main right)

1 2 3 4 5 6 09 08 07 06 05 04

Table of Contents

Birds 4

Birds Are Vertebrates 6

Birds Are Warm-Blooded 8

Bodies of Birds 10

Birds Have Feathers 13

How Birds Breathe 14

What Birds Eat 16

Young Birds 18

Amazing but True! 20
Compare the Main Animal Groups 21
Glossary 22
Read More 23
Internet Sites 23
Index 24

Birds

Birds belong to the animal kingdom. Most birds can fly. Penguins and ostriches can't fly. Some birds, like loons, swim.

Other groups of animals live on earth with birds. Reptiles have thick, dry skin. Amphibians have moist skin. Fish have fins. Insects have six legs. Mammals have hair.

Birds

Mammals

Reptiles

Main Animal Groups

Insects

Amphibians

Fish

Birds Are Vertebrates

Birds are **vertebrates**. Vertebrate animals have backbones. Bones in a bird's **skeleton** join to the backbone.

Most birds have **hollow** areas inside some of their bones. The hollow areas make this bald eagle light enough to fly.

bald eagle

Birds Are Warm-Blooded

Birds are warm-blooded. Their body temperatures stay the same in hot and cold weather. A bird's body turns food into **energy**. Energy keeps this cardinal and other birds warm.

northern cardinal

Bodies of Birds

All birds have the same body parts as this indigo bunting. Birds have a head with two eyes and a **bill**. Birds have two wings, two legs, and two feet.

indigo bunting

Somali ostrich

Most birds have **scales** and four toes on each foot. Ostriches are the only birds with two toes on each foot. Scales protect a bird's foot.

mallard

Birds Have Feathers

Birds have skin covered with feathers. Birds are the only animals that have feathers. Feathers help birds fly. Colorful feathers help some birds find mates. Feathers also keep birds warm. Waterproof feathers keep a mallard's body dry.

Fun Fact!
Feathers are made of keratin. Human hair and fingernails are also made of keratin.

How Birds Breathe

Falcons and other birds breathe in air through their nose and mouth. The air first goes into two **lungs**. The air then moves into air **sacs**. Some of the sacs store air. When birds breathe out, the stored air goes back into the lungs. Birds always have fresh air in their lungs because of the air sacs.

Fun Fact!

Birds can't sweat to stay cool. Instead, air moves between their air sacs and lungs. The air helps keep their heart and other important organs cool.

peregrine falcon

15

scarlet macaw

What Birds Eat

Birds eat many kinds of food. Some birds eat seeds, fruit, or worms. This macaw opens a seed with its bill.

saw-whet owl

Some birds swoop down to the ground to catch animals. This owl uses its feet to grab a mouse.

Young Birds

Birds **hatch** from eggs. Most newly hatched birds are blind and cannot stand. They stay in a nest until they can fly. Most birds bring food to their offspring. Robins feed worms to their chicks. The chicks quickly grow up and leave the nest.

Fun Fact!
Chicks have soft feathers called down on their bodies.

Amazing but True!

The hummingbird is the world's smallest bird. It is the only bird that can fly backward. It also can fly straight up, sideways, and upside down. Hummingbirds can flap their tiny wings at least 70 times in one second.

Compare the Main Animal Groups

	Vertebrates	Invertebrates	Warm-blooded	Cold-blooded	Hair	Feathers	Scales
Birds	X		X			X	
Amphibians	X			X			
Fish	X			X			X
Insects		X		X			
Mammals	X		X		X		
Reptiles	X			X			X

Glossary

bill (BILL)—the hard, pointed part of a bird's mouth

energy (EN-ur-jee)—the ability to do work; food energy in a bird's body works to keep it warm.

hatch (HACH)—to break out of an egg

hollow (HOL-oh)—having nothing inside

lungs (LUHNGS)—organs inside the chest that animals use to breathe; air goes in and out of the lungs when animals breathe.

sac (SAK)—a body part shaped like a bag that can store air or fluid

scales (SKALES)—small, hard pieces of skin

skeleton (SKEL-uh-tuhn)—the bones that support and protect the body

vertebrate (VUR-tuh-bruht)—an animal that has a backbone

22

Read More

Heinrichs, Ann. *Birds.* Nature's Friends. Minneapolis: Compass Point Books, 2003.

McEvoy, Paul. *Birds.* Animal Facts. Philadelphia: Chelsea Clubhouse Books, 2003.

Unwin, Mike. *The Life Cycle of Birds.* From Egg to Adult. Chicago: Heinemann Library, 2003.

Internet Sites

FactHound offers a safe, fun way to find Internet sites related to this book. All of the sites on FactHound have been researched by our staff.

Here's how:
1. Visit *www.facthound.com*
2. Type in this special code **0736826211** for age-appropriate sites. Or enter a search word related to this book for a more general search.
3. Click on the **Fetch It** button.

FactHound will fetch the best sites for you!

Index

bald eagles, 6
bills, 10, 16
breathing, 14

cardinals, 8
chicks, 18

eggs, 18
energy, 8

falcons, 14
feathers, 13, 18
feet, 10, 11, 17
food, 16–17, 18

hatch, 18
hummingbirds, 20

indigo buntings, 10

legs, 4, 10
loons, 4
lungs, 14

macaws, 16
mallards, 13
mouths, 14

nests, 18
noses, 14

ostriches, 4, 11
owls, 17

penguins, 4

robins, 18

sacs, 14
seeds, 16
skeleton, 6

toes, 11

vertebrates, 6

warm-blooded, 8
wings, 10, 20